To Parents and Teachers

This book was written to help middle and older elementary children become familiar with their Bibles and learn how to use them.

This is a self-instruction book, designed for a student to use alone at his or her own speed. To use the book, the student needs a CEB (Common English Bible), preferably the Deep Blue Kids Bible, published by Abingdon Press (© 2012, Nashville, Tennessee). The student also needs a pencil with an eraser and a pair of scissors. Each individual needs her or his own copy of this book. The child will need to write answers on the pages where instructed to do so.

Since this book is intended for use with the Abingdon CEB Common English Bible, a student might need assistance if using a different version of the Bible.

Younger, more inexperienced readers will require three to four hours to complete this book, whereas older, more experienced readers might be able to complete this book in one to two hours.

In order to [illegible] dent must be able t[illegible] ge numbers as hig[illegible] e between a con[illegible] hen they are used in a Bib[illegible]

A student who has completed this book will be able to:

- find any book in the Old or New Testaments using the Bible's table of contents;
- find any chapter in any book and any verse in any chapter;
- find parts of verses when the Bible reference uses the letters a, b, and c with a verse number;
- tell the difference between books of the Bible with similar names, such as 1 Samuel and 2 Samuel or John and 1 John;
- recognize the additional helps in a Bible and be able to use them.

This resource can be used in the classroom or at home during any time of day.

In-text Notes

Throughout the Bible there are notes that talk about what the Bible says.

- **Sailboat** notes help us grow stronger with God by pointing out positive traits we can have in our lives.
- **Umbrella** notes give us help for difficult times by explaining how unhappy emotions and traits aren't good for us.
- **Lighthouse** notes help us develop rock solid faith by discussing the basics of following God for life.
- **Life Preserver** notes give us answers to tough questions and hard-to-understand sections of the Bible.

P-6

If you are using the CEB Deep Blue Kids Bible, you will find four icons that will help you better understand what the Bible is saying. The icons are:

1) Sailboat. These notes will help you grow stronger with God by pointing out positive traits in your life.

2) Umbrella. These notes will help you during difficult times by discussing unhappy emotions and traits that aren't good for us.

3) Lighthouse. These notes discuss the basics of following God to help you develop rock-solid faith.

4) Life Preserver. These notes give answers to tough questions and hard-to-understand sections of the Bible.

This book is a different kind of book. It is something like a puzzle book. To use this book, you will need a Common English Bible (CEB). The CEB Deep Blue Kids Bible will be the most helpful. You will also need a pencil with an eraser on it and a pair of scissors.

If you have your Bible, pencil, and scissors, then you can begin using this book.

On each page, you will read something about your Bible.

Then you will read a sentence that has some words missing, or maybe there will be a question.

Sometimes you will write the answer in a blank space like this: ______________________________.

Sometimes your answer will have more than one word, and you will write in spaces like this: __________ __________ __________.

Or the answer may be started for you: a _ _ _ _ _ and you will finish it like this: a n s w e r.

Sometimes you will check the right answer, like this:

_____ wrong answer

_____ right answer

Look in the gray strip at the left side of the next page.

map

HALLELUJAH!
This is the end of the book.

Now you know how to use a Bible.
You know that every Bible is a little different,
but you will know the things you should search for
in any Bible and how to find many things in any Bible.

4

LOOK HERE FOR THE ANSWER:

The right answer will always be found in this gray strip on the left side of the next page after the question.

Don't be surprised if a question is the same as a question you have already answered. Some of the questions will be asked again.

That makes the answers very EASY!

And by thinking of and writing the answer more than once, you will learn it and remember it for a long time.

Many of the questions are not hard but are E __ __ __.

That's it! Take your pencil and write one letter in each blank!

Now look at the left side of the next page to check your answer.

167

bottom

footnote

If you wanted to find where a city, country, lake, river, or sea mentioned in the Bible is located, you would look on a m __ __ found in the Bible.

5

See! You got this answer right!

EASY

Sometimes this book will tell you to look for things in the Bible. Then you will stop reading this book and look in your BIBLE.

When you have found what you are looking for in your Bible, you will come back to this book to see if you have found the right thing.

This book will help you learn to use your B __ __ __ __.

You know that word. It tells the stories of God's people!

Remember to check your answer on the next page.

Dictionary

When you see a little letter (like a, b, h, or m) by a word as you read in the Bible, you know that it tells you to look at the ____________________ of the page if you want to learn more.

When you look there, you will find a ____________________ with more information

Isn't this easy?

BIBLE

But be careful!

In order to learn how to find things in your Bible, be sure to read every line on each page in this book and DO EVERYTHING THE BOOK TELLS YOU TO DO.

By the time you reach the end of this book, you will know how to use your ____________________ very well.

Check your answer.

165

Bible Basics

If you do not understand a certain word in your Bible, you can look in the Bible ____________________.

7

Bible

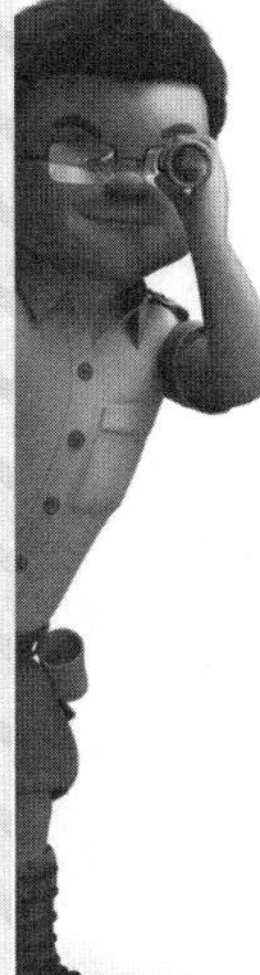

Another different thing about this book is that once you are finished reading all the pages that go this way, then you turn the book around and read the rest of the pages.

This is a very different and interesting book!

Now you are ready to begin learning how to find certain things in your ____________________.
You will learn how to use your ________________ so that you can use it every single day of your life!

First 12

second

31

14

first 1

In the CEB Deep Blue Kids Bible, there is a section in the front of the Bible called B_________ B__________.

This section talks about what the Bible is, who wrote the Bible, when it was written, why the Bible is important to people today, and how you can find your way through the Bible.

The Bible looks like one big book.

Bible

Bible

But it really is a lot of smaller books put together. It is like a library full of books.

Did you know that the word BIBLE means BOOKS?

Another word for "books" is __ __ __ __ __.

First

The Bible reference

1 CORINTHIANS 12:31b through 14:1a

means that you find ____________ Corinthians, Chapter _________.

You begin reading at the _________________ part of verse _________ and read to the end of Chapter 13.

Then you read on into Chapter _________ to the end of the _____________ part of verse ________.

9

Bible

When you say the word "Bible," you are actually talking about a lot of smaller ___ ___ ___ ___ ___ put together into one big book.

162

second

In the Bible reference 1 SAMUEL 3:10, the number 1 in the name means that you are to find ____________________ Samuel.

163

10

books

The word "Bible" means _________________________.

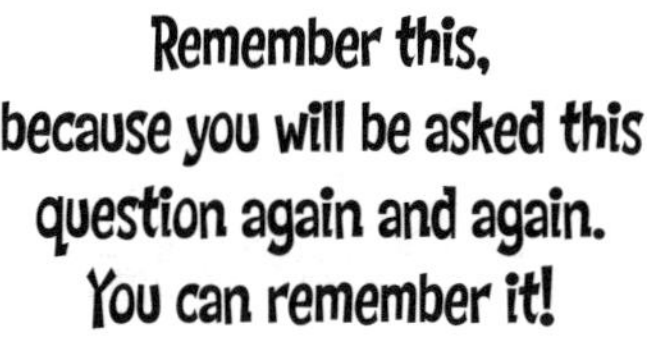

161

first

In the Bible reference MATTHEW 28:20b, the "b" after the "20" means that you read the ____________________ part of verse 20.

11

books

The Bible is called "Bible" because it is not just one big book, it is a lot of smaller

____

with one cover.

1 1 8

19

14 15

In the Bible reference MATTHEW 28:19a, the "a" after the "19" means that you read only the ________________ part of verse 19.

books

The word "Bible" means ________________________.

skip

In the Bible reference JEREMIAH 1:1-8; 19:14-15, first you read Chapter __________, verses ___________ through __________.

Then you skip to Chapter __________ and read verses __________ and __________.

13

books

See! We asked you the same question again. I bet you learned the answer!

This is a picture of a page near the front of the Bible.

Draw a circle around the words in this picture that say COMMON ENGLISH BIBLE.

See if you can find this page in your Bible.

a fresh translation to touch the heart and mind

158

21

37

22 1

In the Bible reference COLOSSIANS 3:17, 23-24
the comma (,) means that you

_____ read all the verses between 17 and 23.

or

_____ skip all the verses between 17 and 23.

14

If you had a hard time finding this page in your Bible, ask someone for help.

If you look at the next few pages in your Bible, you may notice that there are two MAIN PARTS in the Bible: the O__________ and N___________ Testaments.

1 6

read

The Bible reference LUKE 21:37 through 22:1 means that you are to find the Book of Luke, Chapter __________, and begin reading at verse __________.

When you finish that chapter, you keep on reading in Chapter __________ to the end of verse __________.

15

Old New

Can you find how many books of the Bible there are?

____

We have learned that the Bible is a collection of books. These books were stories that people told from memory. Parents told these stories about God's people to their children, who told them to their children. Later, the stories were written down.

Before the stories were written down, how did the stories spread? The stories were told from M __ M __ __ __.

156

verse

In the Bible reference MARK 3:1-6, you read from the beginning of verse __________ to the end of verse __________.

The hyphen (-) means you

_____ read all the verses between 1 and 6.

or

_____ skip all the verses between 1 and 6.

16

66

memory

The Bible is a gift to us from God. As we read the Bible, we learn more about God's great love for all people and how Jesus taught us to live.

The Bible is a gift to us from ___ ___ ___.

The Bible tells us how Jesus wants us to ___ ___ ___ ___.

155

chapter

In the Bible reference LUKE 2:14,
the number "14" is the _____ verse number.
or
_____ chapter number.

17

God

live

The name of one large group of books in the Bible is the OLD Testament.

A second large group of books in the Bible is called the ___________ Testament.

154

verses

In the Bible reference LUKE 2:14

the number "2" is the _____ verse number.

or

_____ chapter number.

(Check the right word.)

155

NEW

A list of the books of the Bible is found in every Bible. Open your Bible. You will have to turn the pages until you find a page that looks like this:

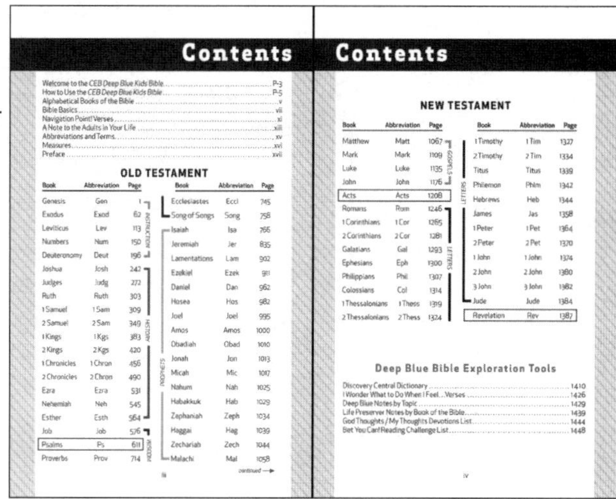

Contents

OLD TESTAMENT

continued →

iii

Contents

NEW TESTAMENT

Deep Blue Bible Exploration Tools

iv

This list of books takes two pages and is in two parts:

The Books of the _______________ Testament

The Books of the _______________ Testament

153

chapters

In the Bible, the chapters have been divided into small parts called ____________________.

154

19

Old or New
New or Old

(Either way is right.)

Now find the name of the SECOND book in the OLD Testament list.

Write that name here: __ __ __ __ __ __

Cut out this bookmark and keep it at the page that says "Contents" at the top.

152

Sailboat

Umbrella

Lighthouse

Life Preserver

Most of the books of the Bible have been divided into large parts called ____________________.

20

Exodus

Now see if you can find the Book of RUTH. It is also in the Old Testament list.

Ruth is _______ eight or _______ ten books down on the Old Testament list.

(Check the right number.)

151

Old

New

or

New

Old

In the CEB Deep Blue Kids Bible, there are four special icons. The four icons are:

1) _ _ _ _boat.

2) _ _ _ _ _ _ _ _.

3) _ _ _ _ _house.

4) _ _ _ _ Preserver.

21

eight

Lay a ruler or a pencil across the page under the name of the Book of Ruth.

In YOUR Bible, the Book of Ruth begins on page __________.

Turn to the Book of Ruth in your Bible, and keep the place.

Did you find the Book of Ruth in YOUR Bible?

Ruth

things **YOU'LL DISCOVER**

Ruth is a story with a sad beginning and a happy ending. At the start, a woman named Ruth and her mother-in-law, Naomi, are hungry and lonely. As their story unfolds, they find not only food but friendship and love.

people **YOU'LL MEET**

Naomi—an Israelite woman and the mother-in-law of Ruth (Ruth 1–4)
Elimelech—Naomi's husband (Ruth 1)
Ruth—a young woman from Moab who married the son of Naomi and Elimelech (Ruth 1–4)
Boaz—an Israelite man who showed kindness to Ruth (Ruth 2–4)

places **YOU'LL GO**

Israel, Moab (present-day Jordan)

words **YOU'LL REMEMBER**

"But Ruth replied, 'Don't urge me to abandon you, to turn back from following after you. Wherever you go, I will go; and wherever you stay, I will stay. Your people will be my people, and your God will be my God.'" (Ruth 1:16)

The book of Ruth tells us how families take care of each other. The story takes place in the days when Israel had tribal leaders, before Israel had a king. Naomi and her husband Elimelech faced famine and hunger in Israel. So they left their home and traveled to the land of Moab to find food. While they were in Moab, their two sons married women from that country.

Eventually, Elimelech died. Then his two sons died. Their three wives were left alone with no family to care for them. In those days it would have been very hard for these women to provide for themselves apart from a family.

Naomi decided to return home to Israel, and Ruth wanted to go with her. Naomi told Ruth to remain with her own people in Moab, but Ruth promised to stay with Naomi no matter what happened. Ruth vowed that Naomi's God would now be her God.

In this book we learn how God led Ruth to a kind man, Boaz, who cared for her and Naomi. At the end of this story, Boaz and Ruth get married. Her story shows us how to be loyal and loving!

150

two

One of these two main parts of the Bible is called the ________________ Testament.

The other main part of the Bible is called the ________________ Testament.

22

Be sure that you found the correct page in your Bible and that you found the Book of Ruth. It might begin on page 304!

Ruth

things
YOU'LL DISCOVER

Ruth is a story with a sad beginning and a happy ending. At the start, a woman named Ruth and her mother-in-law, Naomi, are hungry and lonely. As their story unfolds, they find not only food but friendship and love.

people
YOU'LL MEET

Naomi—an Israelite woman and the mother-in-law of Ruth (Ruth 1–4)
Elimelech—Naomi's husband (Ruth 1)
Ruth—a young woman from Moab who married the son of Naomi and Elimelech (Ruth 1–4)
Boaz—an Israelite man who showed kindness to Ruth (Ruth 2–4)

places
YOU'LL GO

Israel, Moab (present-day Jordan)

words
YOU'LL REMEMBER

"But Ruth replied, 'Don't urge me to abandon you, to turn back from following after you. Wherever you go, I will go; and wherever you stay, I will stay. Your people will be my people, and your God will be my God'" (Ruth 1:16).

The book of Ruth tells us how families take care of each other. The story takes place in the days when Israel had tribal leaders, before Israel had a king. Naomi and her husband Elimelech faced famine and hunger in Israel. So they left their home and traveled to the land of Moab to find food. While they were in Moab, their two sons married women from that country.

Eventually, Elimelech died. Then his two sons died. Their three wives were left alone with no family to care for them. In those days it would have been very hard for these women to provide for themselves apart from a family.

Naomi decided to return home to Israel, and Ruth wanted to go with her. Naomi told Ruth to remain with her own people in Moab, but Ruth promised to stay with Naomi no matter what happened. Ruth vowed that Naomi's God would now be her God.

In this book we learn how God led Ruth to a kind man, Boaz, who cared for her and Naomi. At the end of this story, Boaz and Ruth get married. Her story shows us how to be loyal and loving!

Look at where the story of Ruth begins. Find the words that say, "During the days when the judges ruled, there was a famine in the land. A man with his wife and two sons went from Bethlehem of Judah to dwell in the territory of Moab."

Find the missing word:
"During the ________ when the judges ruled, there was a famine in the land. A man with his wife and two sons went from Bethlehem of Judah to dwell in the territory of Moab."

Sometimes on the page before a book of the Bible begins, there is information about the book that explains when the book was written and who wrote it. Is there a page like that in your Bible?

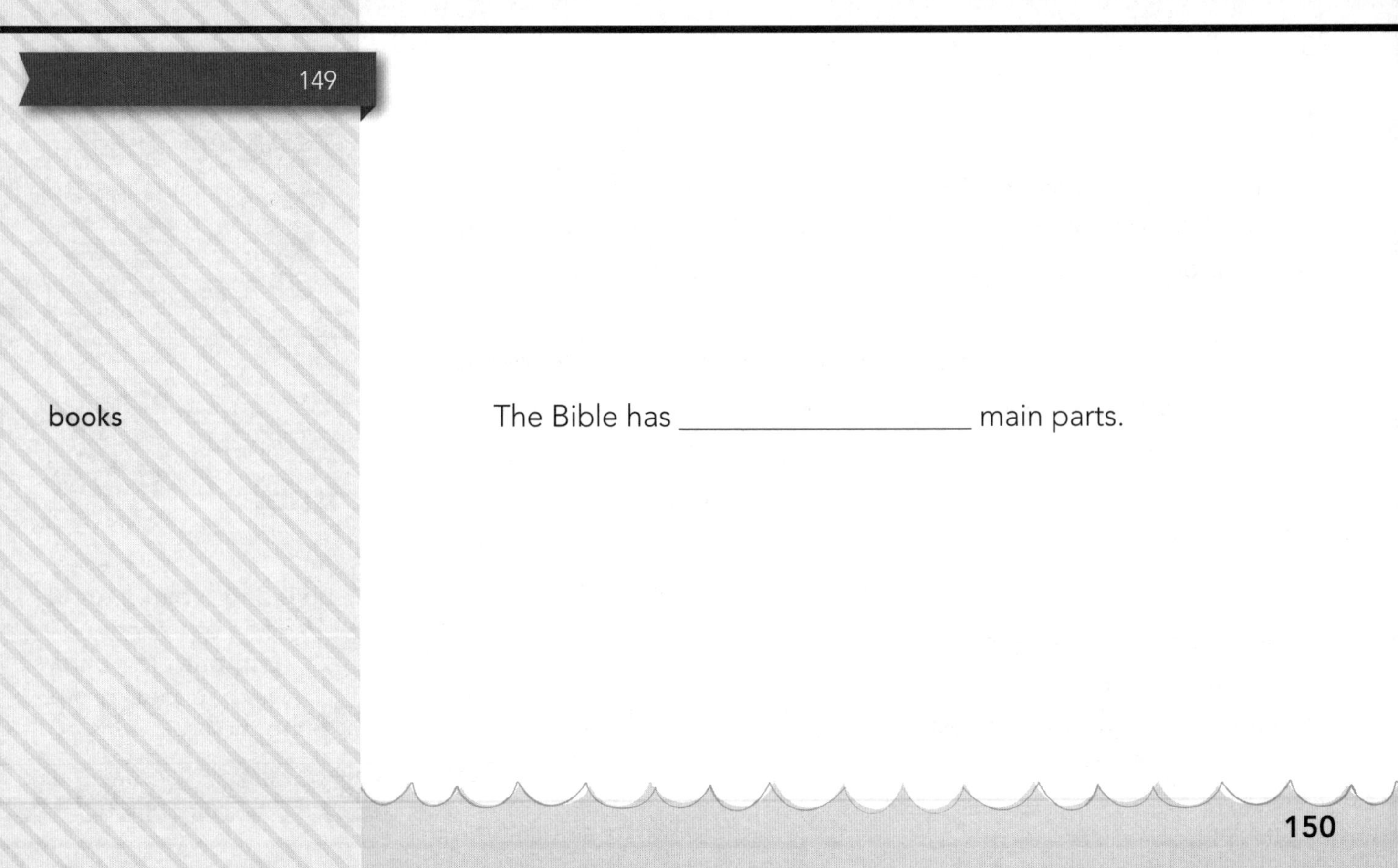

149

books

The Bible has ____________________ main parts.

150

You are learning fast! You have just looked up a book in the Bible!

days

Now let us find another book in the Old Testament. Let us find the Book of JOB.

The name Job sounds like "robe."

Look down the list of books in the front of your Bible until you come to the name "Job."

Find where the actual Book of Job begins.

The Book of Job begins:

"A _______ in the land of Uz was named Job. . . ."

(Fill in the missing word.)

Remember: You might have an introduction page about the Book of Job before the book actually begins.

148

books

The Bible is called the "Bible" because it is not just one big book, it is a lot of smaller ________________ with one cover.

24

man

(If you did not find the Book of Job, look for it again. It is in the Old Testament.)

Let us find one more book in the Old Testament.

See if you can find the Book of JONAH.

The Book of Jonah begins, "The __________ word came to Jonah. . . ."

Remember:
You might have an introduction page about the Book of Jonah before the book actually begins.

The word "Bible" means ______________________________.

LORD'S

(If you did not find the Book of Jonah in your Bible, ask someone to help you before you go any further.)

If you would like to stand up and stretch, this would be a good time.

But first, cut out the bookmark below and put it in this book so you will know where to begin again after you rest.

HOORAY! You've almost reached the end of the book! Rest awhile, and then see how much you remember by answering the questions on the following pages. See how many you get right.

Are you ready to go again?
Let us see what we have learned so far
and then let us learn some more.

The word "Bible" means

______________________________.

145

Good News

The first four books of the New Testament are called the GOSPELS. These books tell us the good news of Jesus Christ.

Write the names of the four Gospels of the New Testament:

____________________ ____________________

____________________ ____________________

books

If you have a CEB Deep Blue Kids Bible by Abingdon Press, you have an icon legend page near the front of your Bible. It shows you that there are four icons (markers) that will tell you something about the story of God and the message of Jesus. Look for these signs:

Sailboat. Grow stronger with God by looking at positive traits in your life!

Umbrella. Learn how truths in the Bible can help you through difficult times!

Do you know what the word GOSPEL means? Read the first two sentences of the information page before the Book of Matthew.

The Gospels tell G__________ N__________, and that is what the word GOSPEL means.

Matthew

T*he first four books of the New Testament—Matthew, Mark, Luke, and John—each tell* exciting stories about Jesus. These books are called *Gospels* because they tell good news about Jesus. Matthew is like a bridge between the Old Testament and the New Testament. This book describes Jesus as the king promised in the Old Testament. It shows how Jesus' teachings compare to the Instruction God gave in the Old Testament.

Matthew tells a lot about Jesus. Men from other countries called magi, searched for him after his birth (Matt 2:1-12). Jesus taught crowds about God (Matt 5–7). He did miraculous acts (Matt 8–9). He predicted his return to earth (Matt 24–25). Jesus died on a cross and rose from the dead (Matt 26:1–28:15). Then he sent his followers to tell the world about him (Matt 28:16-20).

In this book Jesus often calls himself the Human One. He also calls himself God's Son (Matt 27:43). He came so people could experience God's kingdom. When Jesus was about to begin preaching, his cousin John the Baptist shouted, "Here comes the kingdom of heaven!" (Matt 3:2).

things YOU'LL DISCOVER

Matthew tells the story of the arrival of Jesus the king. This book tells all about Jesus, starting with his family history and birth and ending with his death and resurrection.

people YOU'LL MEET

Jesus—the Human One (Matt 1–28)
Mary and Joseph—the mother and father of Jesus (Matt 1–2)
John the Baptist—a prophet who prepared people to meet Jesus (Matt 3; 11; 14)
The Twelve—Jesus' closest disciples, including Peter, James, and John (Matt 4–28)
Pharisees—Jewish religious leaders (Matt 3–27)

places YOU'LL GO

Nazareth (a town in northern Israel),
Jordan River,
Galilee (a lake and region in northern Israel),
Jerusalem,
Skull Place (the site outside Jerusalem where Jesus was crucified)

words YOU'LL REMEMBER

"You must love the Lord your God with all your heart, with all your being, and with all your mind. This is the first and greatest commandment. And the second is like it: You must love your neighbor as you love yourself" (Matt 22:37-39).

Lighthouse. Deepen your faith and focus on the basics of following God!

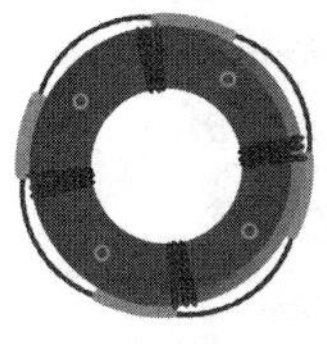

Life Preserver. Find answers to tough questions about the Bible!

The Bible has __________ main parts.

One of these two main parts of the Bible is called the __________ Testament.

musical

Let's find the Book of Matthew in your Bible. In many Bibles, including the CEB Deep Blue Kids Bible, there is a page that gives information about the book. See if you can find the introduction page before the Book of Matthew begins. This page tells what the book is about, lists some of the people in it, and offers other facts to help prepare you to read the book.

29

two

Old or New
(Either one is correct.)

Now find the last book in the Old Testament.
Find the Book of MALACHI.
The Book of Malachi begins:
"A pronouncement. The LORD's ___________ . . ."

(Keep your Bible open to the Book of Malachi.)

142

Dictionary

Let' s find a word in your Bible Dictionary.

Look up the word HARP in your Bible Dictionary.

A HARP is:

A stringed ____________________ instrument small enough to be carried.

word

Your Bible is open to the Book of Malachi, the last book in the Old Testament.

If you turn about five pages (depending on your version of the Bible), you will find a page that looks something like this:

141

Answers will vary depending on your Bible. In the CEB Deep Blue Kids Bible, the answer is 16.

A Bible DICTIONARY tells you what some of the words in the Bible mean.

If you do not understand a word, look in the Bible DICTIONARY to find what it means.

If you do not understand a word in your Bible, you can look in the Bible D ___ ___ ___ ___ ___ ___ ___ ___ ___.

31

You found a page that looks something like this:

In many Bibles, the New Testament starts over again with page 1 and has another set of page numbers. In the CEB Deep Blue Kids Bible, the numbers keep going, so the New Testament begins on page 1065.

Cut out this bookmark and keep it at the page that says "New Testament."

When you want to find a book in the New Testament, this bookmark will show you where to begin looking.

A DICTIONARY is a special book that tells you what words mean.

Many Bibles have a dictionary.

How many pages in your Bible are dictionary pages? ____________

Be sure you put the bookmark at the page that says "The New Testament." Let the bookmark stick out a bit so you can find the page easily.

The first book in the NEW Testament is the Book of

_______________________.

Now look up Genesis 24:22. In this verse, there are two references to shekels. Look for the meaning of this word on the Measures page.

Matthew

Turn to the Book of MATTHEW in your Bible.

If your Bible has an introduction page just before the beginning of the Book of Matthew, you will find information telling you that the Book of Matthew is referred to as a G ___ S ___ E ___.

138

Joanna

Gamaliel

Some Bibles include a chart of Measures. This is where you would go to find out the meaning of an unfamiliar unit of measurement in the Bible.

Look up Exodus 16:33. Then look for your Bible's Measures table (in the CEB Deep Blue Kids Bible, this is a page near the front) and find the word "omer."

139

34

Gospel

Now find another NEW Testament book.

Find the Book of ROMANS.

At the beginning of the Book of Romans, you will find information that says this book of the Bible was a letter that Paul wrote to the church in Rome.

This book is sometimes referred to as:

The Letter of P ___ u ___ to the R ___ m ___ n ___.

Quite often, study helps in a Bible point out useful facts about Bible people. Look up Luke 8:1-3. Does your Bible tell you anything extra about the women mentioned there? One of them was named J ___ ___ ___ ___ A. She is also named in Luke 24:1-12.

The Bible gives us the name of one of Paul's teachers. Look in Acts 22:3. What was the name of the man?

____

See if your Bible study helps offer any more information about him.

35

Paul Romans

Sometimes two or more books in the Bible have almost the same name, like 1 SAMUEL and 2 SAMUEL. (We say "First Samuel" and "Second Samuel.")

The number at the front of the book helps you tell them apart. Look up the Old Testament book 1 SAMUEL.

Be careful! Watch for the number 1 in the name.

Do you remember how we say 1 SAMUEL?

__________ Samuel

sling

nets

Ten Commandments

Sometimes in Bibles, very important parts of the Bible or very important teachings of Jesus are in a special place for people to read, at the end of the Bible or between the Old and New Testaments. One important prayer that Jesus taught is the Lord's Prayer. You can find the Lord' s Prayer in M __ T __ H __ W 6:9-13. In some Bibles it is also printed on a special page all by itself. Read it out loud. Say it every night before you go to sleep, and think about what it means.

Do you know what the Beatitudes are? They are special teachings of Jesus that tell us how to be happy. You can find the BEATI __ __ __ __ __ in Matthew 5:3-12. Sometimes they are given their own special page too. Think about what the Beatitudes mean.

Now look up the book 2 SAMUEL.

Notice that it follows 1 SAMUEL.

Do you remember how we say 2 SAMUEL?

_______________ Samuel

Now you know that there are two books of Samuel:

__________ Samuel

and

__________ Samuel

First

135

lyre

alabaster

When David met Goliath face-to-face in 1 SAMUEL 17:40, he had a ______________ and five stones.

If you look in MARK 1:16-19, you will see that fishermen used fishing ___________.

If you look in EXODUS 20:1-17, you will find the T__ __ ________________________.

Second

1 or First

2 or Second

How do you SAY the name of the book 1 SAMUEL?

Check the right answer:

_____ One Samuel

_____ First Samuel

How do you SAY the name of the book 2 SAMUEL?

_____ Second Samuel

_____ Two Samuel

maps

If you have a CEB Deep Blue Kids Bible, you can find some of these study helps in your Bible. They are found in a section called Exploration Tools. Turn to the Book of Revelation. It is the last book of the Bible. After the end of Revelation, you will find many pages of study helps. First there is a dictionary that can tell you more about objects, people, and ideas you find in Bible verses, like the ones that follow.

If you look in 1 SAMUEL 16:23, you will see that David played the ______________ before King Saul. A lyre was a musical instrument, much like a harp.

If you look in MARK 14:3, you will find that a woman poured perfume on Jesus' head from a vase made of ________________, a kind of stone.

38

First

Second

When you see the name of the book 2 SAMUEL, you know that the number 2 in the name means that you are to find ________________ Samuel (2 Samuel) instead of FIRST Samuel (1 Samuel).

133

Bible Basics

What is the Bible?

The Bible is a very special collection of books (or scrolls) filled with stories of God's love for people. These sixty-six books tell about God, the creator of the universe who made people and wants them to follow God's ways. God loves people and sent Jesus to be the savior of the people of the whole world. The books in the Bible show us what God is like and how we can know God. The Bible comes from God, who inspired people to write down God's teaching. *Inspire* means that God's Spirit breathed through the writers who wrote the books. God also inspires us to read and understand those same teachings. Throughout history and still today the Bible changes people's lives.

Who wrote the Bible, and when was it written?

This collection of books was written by many different people. A long time ago there weren't written Bible stories. For hundreds of years, people told their children the stories from memory and those children told the same stories to their children. About 950 years before Jesus, people began writing down the stories and teachings found in the Old Testament in the Hebrew language.

The stories and teachings in the New Testament were also told for many years before they were written. Some of the letters were written about twenty-five years after Jesus died. About five years later, people started writing down in the Greek language the stories and teachings of Jesus that are called *Gospels*: the books of Matthew, Mark, Luke, and John.

Why is the Bible important to people today?

As we read our Bibles, we learn more about God's great love for all people and about how Jesus taught us to live. God inspires us to read and understand the Bible for ourselves. The Bible shows us how awesome God is and how we can know God!

POP QUIZ

Is the Bible a single book? Why or why not?

How can I find my way through the Bible?

The Bible is like a library you can hold in your hand. Each book has its own name and place in the Bible library. Different books of the Bible library have different kinds of writings. Some give God's Instruction. Others tell stories of history. Some are songs or poems. Others contain warnings. Some tell about Jesus. Others are letters to individuals or groups of people.

vii

Many times you will want to see where a city, town, river, or sea is located. You can find these places on a map. Finding these places might help you understand a Bible story better. You will definitely need a Bible MAP.

Maps in Bibles can be found in several locations. Often they are at the front or the back of a Bible.

Most Bibles have ______________ to help you find where a city, town, river, or sea is located.

Second

There is a book in the New Testament called 1 PETER.

Remember, we SAY "First Peter."

There is another book in the New Testament with a name very much like 1 PETER. Can you guess its name? Try, and write it here:

_____ ________________

footnotes

Most Bibles have extra pages called STUDY HELPS or BIBLE BASICS that give information about the Bible, how the Bible was written, why the Bible is important to people today, how to find one's way through the Bible, a description of the books of the Bible, how to find specific Bible verses or passages, or what is a good way to begin reading the Bible.

Here is a picture of BIBLE BASICS from the front of the Deep Blue Kids Bible. Draw a circle around the words BIBLE BASICS.

Bible Basics

What is the Bible?

The Bible is a very special collection of books (or scrolls) filled with stories of God's love for people. These sixty-six books tell about God, the creator of the universe who made people and wants them to follow God's ways. God loves people and sent Jesus to be the savior of the people of the whole world. The books in the Bible show us what God is like and how we can know God. The Bible comes from God, who inspired people to write down God's teaching. *Inspire* means that God's Spirit breathed through the writers who wrote the books. God also inspires us to read and understand those same teachings. Throughout history and still today the Bible changes people's lives.

Who wrote the Bible, and when was it written?

This collection of books was written by many different people. A long time ago there weren't written Bible stories. For hundreds of years, people told their children the stories from memory and those children told the same stories to their children. About 950 years before Jesus, people began writing down the stories and teachings found in the Old Testament in the Hebrew language.

The stories and teachings in the New Testament were also told for many years before they were written. Some of the letters were written about twenty-five years after Jesus died. About five years later, people started writing down in the Greek language the stories and teachings of Jesus that are called *Gospels*: the books of Matthew, Mark, Luke, and John.

Why is the Bible important to people today?

As we read our Bibles, we learn more about God's great love for all people and about how Jesus taught us to live. God inspires us to read and understand the Bible for ourselves. The Bible shows us how awesome God is and how we can know God!

POP QUIZ

Is the Bible a single book? Why or why not?

How can I find my way through the Bible?

The Bible is like a library you can hold in your hand. Each book has its own name and place in the Bible library. Different books of the Bible library have different kinds of writings. Some give God's Instruction. Others tell stories of history. Some are songs or poems. Others contain warnings. Some tell about Jesus. Others are letters to individuals or groups of people.

vii

2 Peter

Now turn again to the NEW Testament list of books.

In the New Testament list, you will see that more than one book has the word "John" in its name, but they are not all together in the list.

How many books in the New Testament have the word "John" in their name? _______________

131

bottom

The little notes at the bottom of the page that give more information are called ____________________.

41

Four

(Look until you find all four.)

Find the book JOHN in your Bible. It is in the New Testament list.

Be careful! Find JOHN, not 1 JOHN (First John).

130

bottom

footnote

FOOTNOTES are little notes that give you more information.

Footnotes are found at the ________________ of the page.

Now find the book 1 JOHN.

Do we say:

______ First John

or

______ One John?

129

Isa 40:3; Mal 3:1; Exod 23:20

When you see a little letter (like a, b, h, or m) by a word as you read in the Bible, you know it tells you to look at the

_____ top of the page.

or

_____ bottom of the page.

There you will find a f__________.

First

Find the book 2 JOHN.

Remember,
we say,
"Second John."
It comes right after 1 JOHN.

128

footnote

Look up MARK 1:3 in your Bible. This little a in verse 3 means "look for FOOTNOTE a."

Now see if you can find footnote a at the bottom of the page. Footnote a tells more about verse 3.

Footnote a says:

"______________________________"

You know that 1 JOHN and 2 JOHN are not the same book.

The NUMBER at the front of the book helps you know which book you want.

When two or more books in the Bible have almost the same name, you can tell them apart by the n ___ ___ ___ ___ ___.

Let's rest!
(After you check your answer.)
Remember your bookmark.

First

12

second

31

14

first 1

Now, let's learn about small letters that mean something else.

Here is a picture of the beginning of the Gospel of Mark. There is a small a on this page.

These little letters mean "look at the BOTTOM of the page" for a footnote if you want to learn more.

At the bottom of the page is another small a with more information about certain words in verse 3.

This extra information at the bottom of the page is called a

___ ___ ___ ___ ___ ___ ___ ___.

Mark 1:1 .... 1110 ....

Beginning of good news

1 The beginning of the good news about Jesus Christ, God's Son, [2]happened just as it was written about in the prophecy of Isaiah:

Look, I am sending my messenger
before you.
He will prepare your way,
[3]*a voice shouting in the wilderness:*
"Prepare the way for the Lord;
make his paths straight."[a]

John's preaching

[4]John was in the wilderness calling for people to be baptized to show that they were changing their hearts and lives and wanted God to forgive their sins. [5]Everyone in Judea and all the people of Jerusalem went out to the Jordan River and were being baptized by John as they confessed their sins. [6]John wore clothes made of camel's hair, with a leather belt around his waist. He ate locusts and wild honey. [7]He announced, "One stronger than I am is coming after me. I'm not even worthy to bend over and loosen the strap of his sandals. [8]I baptize you with water, but he will baptize you with the Holy Spirit."

SAILBOAT

HUMILITY

Humility Mark 1:7

Sometimes when people become famous they focus on staying famous. John the Baptist did the opposite. People came from all around to see and hear him, but he wasn't interested in staying well known. Instead, he told everyone that someone even greater was coming. John said that the one who was coming was so incredible that John wasn't even good enough to help him take his shoes off. Helping people remove their shoes when they entered a house was the job of the lowest-ranking servants in the house. It was a job nobody wanted. John knew what job God had given him, and he did it with humility.

Jesus is baptized and tempted

[9]About that time, Jesus came from Nazareth of Galilee, and John baptized him in the Jordan River. [10]While he was coming up out of the water, Jesus saw heaven splitting open and the Spirit, like a dove, coming down on him. [11]And there was a voice from heaven: "You are my Son, whom I dearly love; in you I find happiness."

[12]At once the Spirit forced Jesus out into the wilderness. [13]He was in the wilderness for forty days, tempted by Satan. He was among the wild animals, and the angels took care of him.

Jesus' message

[14]After John was arrested, Jesus came into Galilee announcing God's good news, [15]saying, "Now is the time! Here comes God's kingdom! Change your hearts and lives, and trust this good news!"

Jesus calls disciples

[16]As Jesus passed alongside the Galilee Sea, he saw two brothers, Simon and Andrew, throwing fishing nets into the sea, for they were fishermen. [17]"Come, follow me," he said, "and I'll show you how to fish for people." [18]Right away, they left their nets and followed him. [19]After going a little farther, he saw James and John, Zebedee's sons, in their boat repairing the fishing nets. [20]At that very moment he called them. They followed him, leaving their father Zebedee in the boat with the hired workers.

Jesus throws a demon out

[21]Jesus and his followers went into Capernaum. Immediately on the Sabbath Jesus entered the synagogue and started teaching. [22]The people were amazed by his teaching, for he was teaching them with authority, not like the legal experts. [23]Suddenly, there in the synagogue, a person with an evil spirit screamed, [24]"What have you to do with us, Jesus of Nazareth? Have you come to destroy us? I know who you are. You are the holy one from God."

[25]"Silence!" Jesus said, speaking harshly

did you know? When Jesus was baptized, Mark said the Holy Spirit came down like a dove to where Jesus was. This is why the dove is a symbol of the Holy Spirit in the church.

[a]Isa 40:3; Mal 3:1; Exod 23:20

number

In many Bibles, there is a dictionary. Often the dictionary is in the back of the Bible.

Does your Bible have a dictionary?

Is it in the front or the back of your Bible?

See if you can find the words "Jesus Christ" in your dictionary. Can you read what it says about Jesus Christ out loud?

We'll return to the dictionary later in this book. For now, let's look at Bible references.

Who

king

The reference

1 CORINTHIANS 12:31b through 14:1a

means that you find ______________ Corinthians, Chapter ______________.

You begin reading there at the ______________ part of verse __________ and read to the end of Chapter 13.

Then you read on into Chapter __________ to the end of the ______________ part of verse __________.

That was a lot of work, wasn't it? Check your answers on the next page and then stop and take a rest. You deserve it!

46

Now that you know how to find any book in the Bible, you are ready to learn how to find any part of any book in the Bible.

A Bible REFERENCE (pronounced “REF er ens”) tells you where to look to find a part of a book in the Bible.

If your teacher says, “Look up John three-sixteen,” she or he is giving you a Bible refer ___ ___ ___ ___.

125

God

made

Look up PSALM 24:8a in your Bible.
Write the first word of Psalm 24:8a here: __________
Write the last word of Psalm 24:8a here: __________________.
(Did you look up the FIRST part of PSALM 24:8?)

reference

Your teacher would WRITE the reference like this:

JOHN 3:16

(She or he would SAY, "John three-sixteen.")

The first thing a Bible reference tells you is which BOOK in the Bible you are to look up.

In the reference JOHN 3:16, the word "John" is the name of the ________________ you are to find.

124

first

Look up PSALM 100:3a, b in your Bible.

It says,

"Know that the Lord is ______________—

he ______________ us; we belong to him."

(This Bible reference tells you to read ONLY the first and second parts of verse 3, even though the verse has more than two parts.)

This is a picture of the beginning of the Book of John. The big number 1 means "Chapter 1 begins here."

Circle the big number 1 in this picture.

book

Story of the Word

1 In the beginning was the Word
and the Word was with God
and the Word was God.
2 The Word was with God
in the beginning.
3 Everything came into being
through the Word,
and without the Word
nothing came into being.
What came into being
4 through the Word was life,[a]
and the life was the light for all people.
5 The light shines in the darkness,
and the darkness doesn't
extinguish the light.
6 A man named John was sent from God.
7 He came as a witness to testify concerning
the light, so that through him everyone would
believe in the light. 8 He himself wasn't the
light, but his mission was to testify concerning the light.
9 The true light that shines on all people
was coming into the world.
10 The light was in the world,
and the world came into being
through the light,
but the world didn't recognize
the light.
11 The light came to his own people,
and his own people didn't welcome him.
12 But those who did welcome him,
those who believed in his name,
he authorized to become God's children,
13 born not from blood
nor from human desire or passion,
but born from God.
14 The Word became flesh
and made his home among us.
We have seen his glory,
glory like that of a father's only son,
full of grace and truth.
15 John testified about him, crying out,
"This is the one of whom I said, 'He who comes
after me is greater than me because he ex-
isted before me.'"
16 From his fullness we have all received
grace upon grace;
17 as the Law was given through Moses,
so grace and truth came into being
through Jesus Christ.
18 No one has ever seen God.
God the only Son,
who is at the Father's side,
has made God known.

Bet you can read this in 30 seconds. Ready, set, go!

LIFE PRESERVER

What is "the Word"?

John 1:1-5

John is very different from Matthew, Mark, and Luke. John's Gospel was written later than the other three. John tells some different stories about Jesus and uses a lot of images like bread, water, light, and vines.

This book begins without a family tree (see Matthew), Jesus' baptism (see Mark), or a birth story (see Luke). Instead, it begins with the Story *of the Word*. John told his readers that Jesus is God's Word and work in the world. Jesus is God's presence in the world. God became human through the birth, life, death, and resurrection of Jesus. Then John shares stories that support his statement of who Jesus is.

John's witness

19 This is John's testimony when the Jewish
leaders in Jerusalem sent priests and Levites
to ask him, "Who are you?"
20 John confessed (he didn't deny but confessed), "I'm not the Christ."
21 They asked him, "Then who are you? Are
you Elijah?"
John said, "I'm not."
"Are you the prophet?"
John answered, "No."
22 They asked, "Who are you? We need to
give an answer to those who sent us. What do
you say about yourself?"
23 John replied,
"I am a voice crying out in the wilderness,
Make the Lord's path straight,[b]
just as the prophet Isaiah said."
24 Those sent by the Pharisees 25 asked,
"Why do you baptize if you aren't the Christ,
nor Elijah, nor the prophet?"
26 John answered, "I baptize with water.

[a]*Or Everything came into being through the Word,/and without the Word / nothing came into being that came into being. In the Word was life* [b]Isa 40:3

123

second

124

If you were told, "Keep on reading through verse 8a," that would mean you would stop after reading the ____________ part of verse 8.

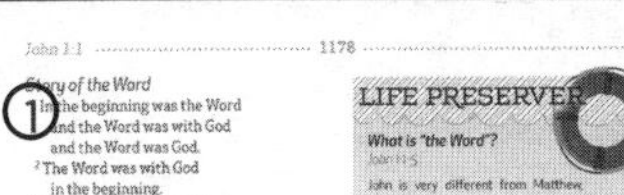

John 1:1 .... 1178 ....

Story of the Word

1 In the beginning was the Word
and the Word was with God
and the Word was God.
2 The Word was with God
in the beginning.
3 Everything came into being
through the Word,
and without the Word
nothing came into being.
What came into being
4 through the Word was life,[a]
and the life was the light for all people.
5 The light shines in the darkness,
and the darkness doesn't
extinguish the light.
6 A man named John was sent from God.
7 He came as a witness to testify concerning
the light, so that through him everyone would
believe in the light. 8 He himself wasn't the
light, but his mission was to testify concerning the light.
9 The true light that shines on all people
was coming into the world.
10 The light was in the world,
and the world came into being
through the light,
but the world didn't recognize
the light.
11 The light came to his own people,
and his own people didn't welcome him.
12 But those who did welcome him,
those who believed in his name,
he authorized to become God's children,
13 born not from blood
nor from human desire or passion,
but born from God.
14 The Word became flesh
and made his home among us.
We have seen his glory,
glory like that of a father's only son,
full of grace and truth.
15 John testified about him, crying out,
"This is the one of whom I said, 'He who comes
after me is greater than me because he ex-
isted before me.'"
16 From his fullness we have all received
grace upon grace;
17 as the Law was given through Moses,

Bet you can read this in 30 seconds. **Ready, set, go!**

LIFE PRESERVER

What is "the Word"?
John 1:1-5

John is very different from Matthew, Mark, and Luke. John's Gospel was written later than the other three. John tells some different stories about Jesus and uses a lot of images like bread, water, light, and vines.

This book begins without a family tree (see Matthew), Jesus' baptism (see Mark), or a birth story (see Luke). Instead, it begins with the *Story of the Word*. John told his readers that Jesus is God's Word and work in the world. Jesus is God's presence in the world. God became human through the birth, life, death, and resurrection of Jesus. Then John shares stories that support his statement of who Jesus is.

so grace and truth came into being
through Jesus Christ.
18 No one has ever seen God.
God the only Son,
who is at the Father's side,
has made God known.

John's witness

19 This is John's testimony when the Jewish
leaders in Jerusalem sent priests and Levites
to ask him, "Who are you?"
20 John confessed (he didn't deny but confessed), "I'm not the Christ."
21 They asked him, "Then who are you? Are
you Elijah?"
John said, "I'm not."
"Are you the prophet?"
John answered, "No."
22 They asked, "Who are you? We need to
give an answer to those who sent us. What do
you say about yourself?"
23 John replied,
"*I am a voice crying out in the wilderness,*
Make the Lord's path straight,[b]
just as the prophet Isaiah said."
24 Those sent by the Pharisees 25 asked,
"Why do you baptize if you aren't the Christ,
nor Elijah, nor the prophet?"
26 John answered, "I baptize with water.

[a]Or *Everything came into being through the Word,/and without the Word / nothing came into being that came into being. In the Word was life* [b]Isa 40:3

Most of the books of the Bible have been divided into large parts called CHAPTERS.

The beginning of each ________________ is marked with a BIG number.

122

first

In a Bible reference like PSALM 33:5b, the "b" after the "5" means that you read the ________________ part of verse 5.

50

chapter

The beginning of the FIRST CHAPTER of a book in the Bible is marked with a big number __________.

Psalm 100

A psalm of thanks.

[1]Shout triumphantly to the LORD,
all the earth!
[2]Serve the LORD with celebration!
Come before him
with shouts of joy!
[3]Know that the LORD is God—
he made us; we belong to him.[k]
We are his people,
the sheep of his own pasture.
[4]Enter his gates with thanks;
enter his courtyards with praise!
Thank him! Bless his name!
[5]Because the LORD is good,
his loyal love lasts forever;
his faithfulness lasts
generation after generation.

Bet you can *read this in 30 seconds.* **Ready, set, go!**

In the Bible reference MATTHEW 28:19a
the "a" after the "19" means that you read only the
________________ part of verse 19.

1

The big number 1 shows you where
C ___ ___ ___ ___ ___ ___ 1 begins.

Psalm 100

A psalm of thanks.

[1] Shout triumphantly to the LORD,
all the earth!
[2] Serve the LORD with celebration!
Come before him
with shouts of joy!
[3] Know that the LORD is God—
he made us; we belong to him.[k]
We are his people,
the sheep of his own pasture.
[4] Enter his gates with thanks;
enter his courtyards with praise!
Thank him! Bless his name!
[5] Because the LORD is good,
his loyal love lasts forever;
his faithfulness lasts
generation after generation.

Bet you can *read this in 30 seconds. Ready, set, go!*

In this picture, draw a circle around all the words of PSALM 100:5a.

Psalm 100

A psalm of thanks.

[1] Shout triumphantly to the LORD,
all the earth!
[2] Serve the LORD with celebration!
Come before him
with shouts of joy!
[3] Know that the LORD is God—
he made us; we belong to him.[k]
We are his people,
the sheep of his own pasture.
[4] Enter his gates with thanks;
enter his courtyards with praise!
Thank him! Bless his name!
[5] Because the LORD is good,
his loyal love lasts forever;
his faithfulness lasts
generation after generation.

Bet you can *read this in 30 seconds. Ready, set, go!*

Be sure you circle only verse 5, part a.

52

Chapter

In a Bible reference, the first number AFTER the name of the book tells you which chapter to look in.

In the reference JOHN 1, the number 1 comes AFTER the name of the book and tells you to look in the first ________________ of the Book of John.

119

b

Here is a picture of PSALM 100.

Psalm 100:2a says, "Serve the Lord with celebration!"

Psalm 100:3b says, "he made us; we belong to him."

Draw a circle around all the words of PSALM 100:3c in the picture.

Psalm 100

A psalm of thanks.

Bet you can ***read this in 30 seconds. Ready, set, go!***

1 Shout triumphantly to the LORD,
all the earth!
2 Serve the LORD with celebration!
Come before him
with shouts of joy!
3 Know that the LORD is God—
he made us; we belong to him.[k]
We are his people,
the sheep of his own pasture.
4 Enter his gates with thanks;
enter his courtyards with praise!
Thank him! Bless his name!
5 Because the LORD is good,
his loyal love lasts forever;
his faithfulness lasts
generation after generation.

Remember! You are looking for verse 3, and part c is the THIRD part of the verse.

120

53

Chapter

In a Bible reference, you know which CHAPTER you are to find by looking at:

the first number _______ before the name of the book.

or

the first number _______ after the name of the book.

(Check the right word ["before" or "after"].)

118

first

In Bible references, the FIRST part of a verse is called "a."
The SECOND part of a verse is called "__________."
The THIRD part of a verse is called "c."

after

Remember!
1 JOHN means the book
FIRST JOHN.
JOHN 1 means the book JOHN, Chapter 1.

We write FIRST JOHN this way:

_____ John 1

or

_____ 1 John

117

a

The letter a means "the FIRST part of a verse."
The letter b means "the SECOND part of a verse."
The letter c means "the THIRD part of a verse."

In the Bible reference PSALM 100:2a
the letter a after the number 2 means that you read only the
________________ part of verse 2.

55

1 John

The Bible reference JOHN 1 means:

_____ the Book of John, Chapter 1

_____ First John

1 1

7 15

Sometimes you will be given a reference that tells you to look up only a PART OF A VERSE.

In the Bible reference PSALM 100:2a

the letter a after the number 2 means that you read only the FIRST PART of verse 2.

In the Bible reference Psalm 100:2a, the letter __________ means that you read only the FIRST PART OF VERSE 2.

****

NOTE: You say "Psalms" when you are talking about the whole Book of Psalms. You say "Psalm" when you are talking about one Psalm.

In the word "Psalm," don't SAY the "P." Just say "Salm."

56

the Book of John, Chapter 1

Now turn again in your Bible to the beginning of the Book of John in the New Testament.

Find the BIG number 2 in the Book of John. You may have to look at the next page to find it. This is Chapter 2. (You would write it JOHN 2.)

The first words of Chapter 2 in the Book of John are:
"On the third ______________ . . ."
(Fill in the missing word.)

115

read

skip

read

Sometimes you read verses in more than one chapter in the same book.

A semicolon (;) is used to separate each set of chapter and verse numbers.

In the Bible reference AMOS 1:1; 7:15

(SAY, "Amos one-one and seven-fifteen.")

first you read chapter __________, verse __________, and then you skip to chapter __________, verse __________, in the Book of Amos.

57

day

The big number 2 means ____________________ 2 begins here.

114

14 17

Sometimes you read different groups of verses in one chapter. A comma is also used here between the groups of verses. The comma (,) tells you which verses to skip.

In the reference 1 JOHN 4:7-8, 11-13, you

_____ skip verses 7-8
_____ read verses 7-8

_____ skip verses 9-10
_____ read verses 9-10

_____ skip verses 11-13
_____ read verses 11-13

58

Now find the big number 3 in the Book of John. It may be on the same page as Chapter 2, or you might need to turn the page.

The big number 3 shows you where Chapter 3 begins.

The first words of JOHN 3 are: "There was a ____________________ . . ."

Chapter

113

child

strong

Jesus

Just for fun, look up in your Bible a very important saying of Jesus to his friends.

JOHN 15:14, 17

You will read verses __________ and __________.

59

Pharisee

Now, let's see if you remember!

JOHN 2 means: _____ Second John or
_____ Book of John, Chapter 2

3 JOHN means: _____ Third John or
_____ Book of John, Chapter 3

JOHN 3 means: _____ Third John or
_____ Book of John, Chapter 3

(Check the THREE right answers.)

112

skip

Look up LUKE 2:40, 52 in your Bible.

Fill in the missing words in the verses below:

VERSE 40:

"The ______________ grew up and became ____________________. He was filled with wisdom, and God's favor was on him."

VERSE 52:

"______________ matured in wisdom and years, and in favor with God and with people."

Book of John,
Chapter 2

Third John

Book of John,
Chapter 3

The Ten Commandments are found in the Bible in the Book of Exodus, Chapter 20.

Find EXODUS in your Bible.

Turn to the Book of Exodus and begin looking for the big number 20 that tells you where Chapter 20 begins.

Most Bibles have numbers at the top of each page showing which chapters are on that page. Some Bibles list only the chapters, and other Bibles give you a full reference for the first or last verse on the page.

These numbers can help you find where Chapter 20 is.

EXODUS 20 begins: "Then ____________________ spoke. . . ."

111

In the Bible reference

LUKE 2:40, 52

52 the comma (,) between the verse numbers means that you

_____ read all the verses between verse 40 and verse 52.

_____ skip all the verses between verse 40 and verse 52.

Check the right word.

61

God

The Ten Commandments are also found in the Bible in DEUTERONOMY 5.

Find the fifth chapter of Deuteronomy in your Bible.

Look until you have found the big number 5.

DEUTERONOMY 5 begins: "_______________ called out to all Israel. . . ."

21

37

22

1

O.K. We've had a rest—let's go!

Notice the comma.
NOW That is different!

Here is a tricky kind of Bible reference.

Look at it carefully.

LUKE 2:40, 52

(We SAY, "Luke two, forty and fifty-two.")

The verse numbers in the reference are separated by a comma (,) instead of a hyphen (-).

When you look up this Bible reference, you read ONLY verse 40 AND verse

________________.

You skip all the verses in between.

Moses

Let's check one more time:

3 JOHN means: _____ Book of John, Chapter 3 or
_____ Third John

EXODUS 5 means: _____ Book of Exodus, Chapter 5 or
_____ Fifth Exodus

1 CORINTHIANS means: _____ Book of Corinthians, Chapter 1 or
_____ First Corinthians

Let's rest! Check your answers and take a rest.

109

all

The Bible reference

LUKE 21:37 through 22:1

means that you are to find the Book of Luke, Chapter __________, and begin reading at verse __________.

When you finish that chapter, you keep on reading in Chapter __________ to the end of verse __________.

How about a rest? Check your answers. Remember your bookmark.

Third John

Book of Exodus, Chapter 5

First Corinthians

Here we go again!

This is a picture of the beginning of Chapter 1 of the Book of Genesis.

The part that is circled is called a VERSE. The circled words are VERSE 1.

The little 2 tells you where VERSE 2 begins.

The little 3 tells you where ___ ___ ___ ___ ___ 3 begins.

3 Genesis 1:26

World's creation in seven days

1 When God began to create[a] the heavens and the earth— 2the earth was without shape or form, it was dark over the deep sea, and God's wind swept over the waters— 3God said, "Let there be light." And so light appeared. 4God saw how good the light was. God separated the light from the darkness. 5God named the light Day and the darkness Night.

There was evening and there was morning: the first day.

6God said, "Let there be a dome in the middle of the waters to separate the waters from each other." 7God made the dome and separated the waters under the dome from the waters above the dome. And it happened in that way. 8God named the dome Sky.

There was evening and there was morning: the second day.

9God said, "Let the waters under the sky come together into one place so that the dry land can appear." And that's what happened. 10God named the dry land Earth, and he named the gathered waters Seas. God saw how good it was. 11God said, "Let the earth grow plant life: plants yielding seeds and fruit trees bearing fruit with seeds inside it, each according to its kind throughout the earth." And that's what happened. 12The earth produced plant life: plants yielding seeds, each according to its kind, and trees bearing fruit with seeds inside it, each according to its kind. God saw how good it was.

13There was evening and there was morning: the third day.

14God said, "Let there be lights in the dome of the sky to separate the day from the night. They will mark events, sacred seasons, days, and years. 15They will be lights in the dome of the sky to shine on the earth." And that's what happened. 16God made the stars and two great lights: the larger light to rule over the day and the smaller light to rule over the night. 17God put them in the dome of the sky to shine on the earth, 18to rule over the day and over the night, and to separate the light from the darkness. God saw how good it was.

19There was evening and there was morning: the fourth day.

LIFE PRESERVER

Why are there two stories of creation? Genesis 1:1–2:25

If you read all the way through Genesis 1 and 2, you may be asking why there are two stories of creation. The first story tells us that the world was created in six days and ends with Sabbath, the day God rested. The second story begins with the garden and tells us that the very first thing God created was a human being.

As you read these two stories, notice the different styles of writing. The first story uses a lot of repetition. God is a bit distant and commands creation. The second story reads like we have zoomed in with a camera to get a close-up picture of the characters interacting with each other. God is much more personal and interacts with creation.

These stories are the work of writers who give us their perspectives on the beginning of life. The variety of voices invites us to think in different ways about the story of God, who lovingly created a world for us to live in and enjoy, a world entrusted to our care.

20God said, "Let the waters swarm with living things, and let birds fly above the earth up in the dome of the sky." 21God created the great sea animals and all the tiny living things that swarm in the waters, each according to its kind, and all the winged birds, each according to its kind. God saw how good it was. 22Then God blessed them: "Be fertile and multiply and fill the waters in the seas, and let the birds multiply on the earth."

23There was evening and there was morning: the fifth day.

24God said, "Let the earth produce every kind of living thing: livestock, crawling things, and wildlife." And that's what happened. 25God made every kind of wildlife, every kind of livestock, and every kind of creature that crawls on the ground. God saw how good it was. 26Then God said, "Let us make humanity in our image to resemble us so that they may take charge of the fish of the sea, the birds of the sky, the livestock, all the earth, and all the crawling things on earth."

[a]Or *In the beginning, God created*

all

In a Bible reference, a hyphen is a short line between verse numbers. The word "through" tells you to go on reading into another chapter.

Both the hyphen and the word "through" tell you to read

_____ none of the verses between the numbers.

or

_____ all of the verses between the numbers.

verse

To make it easier to find things in the Bible, the CHAPTERS have been divided into small parts called VERSES.

In the picture of the beginning of the Book of Genesis, draw a circle around ALL the words in VERSE 5.

World's creation in seven days

1 When God began to create[a] the heavens and
the earth— 2 the earth was without shape or
form, it was dark over the deep sea, and God's
wind swept over the waters— 3 God said, "Let
there be light." And so light appeared. 4 God
saw how good the light was. God separated
the light from the darkness. 5 God named the
light Day and the darkness Night.

There was evening and there was morning: the first day.

107

1	18
2	12

Notice the word "through"!

In the Bible reference MATTHEW 1:18 THROUGH 2:12 the word "through" means that you read

_____ none

_____ all

of the verses between Matthew 1:18 and Matthew 2:12.

World's creation in seven days

1 When God began to create[a] the heavens and
the earth— 2 the earth was without shape or
form, it was dark over the deep sea, and God's
wind swept over the waters— 3 God said, "Let
there be light." And so light appeared. 4 God
saw how good the light was. God separated
the light from the darkness. 5 God named the
light Day and the darkness Night.
There was evening and there was morning:
the first day.

The books of the Bible have been divided into large parts called chapters.

Each of the CHAPTERS has been divided into small parts called v____________________.

106

25

37

all

Sometimes a story begins in one chapter and ends in a following chapter.

The Christmas story in Matthew begins at MATTHEW 1:18. It ends with MATTHEW 2:12.

Here is the way the Bible reference is written:

MATTHEW 1:18 through 2:12

You say, "Matthew one-eighteen through two-twelve."

This Bible reference means that you find the Book of Matthew, Chapter _____, and begin reading at verse __________. You keep on reading to the end of that chapter. You read on in the next chapter (Chapter __________) until you finish verse ___________.

verses

This picture shows the beginning of Chapter 1 of the Book of Genesis in your Bible.

The BIG number tells where the ________________ begins.

The LITTLE numbers help us know where each VERSE begins.

World's creation in seven days

1 When God began to create[a] the heavens and the earth— 2the earth was without shape or form, it was dark over the deep sea, and God's wind swept over the waters— 3God said, "Let there be light." And so light appeared. 4God saw how good the light was. God separated the light from the darkness. 5God named the light Day and the darkness Night.

There was evening and there was morning: the first day.

6God said, "Let there be a dome in the middle of the waters to separate the waters from each other." 7God made the dome and separated the waters under the dome from the waters above the dome. And it happened in that way. 8God named the dome Sky.

There was evening and there was morning: the second day.

9God said, "Let the waters under the sky come together into one place so that the dry land can appear." And that's what happened. 10God named the dry land Earth, and he named the gathered waters Seas. God saw how good it was. 11God said, "Let the earth grow plant life: plants yielding seeds and fruit trees bearing fruit with seeds inside it, each according to its kind throughout the earth." And that's what happened. 12The earth produced plant life: plants yielding seeds, each according to its kind, and trees bearing fruit with seeds inside it, each according to its kind. God saw how good it was.

13There was evening and there was morning: the third day.

14God said, "Let there be lights in the dome of the sky to separate the day from the night. They will mark events, sacred seasons, days, and years. 15They will be lights in the dome of the sky to shine on the earth." And that's what happened. 16God made the stars and two great lights: the larger light to rule over the day and the smaller light to rule over the night. 17God put them in the dome of the sky to shine on the earth, 18to rule over the day and over the night, and to separate the light from the darkness. God saw how good it was.

19There was evening and there was morning: the fourth day.

LIFE PRESERVER

Why are there two stories of creation? Genesis 1:1–2:25

If you read all the way through Genesis 1 and 2, you may be asking why there are two stories of creation. The first story tells us that the world was created in six days and ends with Sabbath, the day God rested. The second story begins with the garden and tells us that the very first thing God created was a human being.

As you read these two stories, notice the different styles of writing. The first story uses a lot of repetition. God is a bit distant and commands creation. The second story reads like we have zoomed in with a camera to get a close-up picture of the characters interacting with each other. God is much more personal and interacts with creation.

These stories are the work of writers who give us their perspectives on the beginning of life. The variety of voices invites us to think in different ways about the story of God, who lovingly created a world for us to live in and enjoy, a world entrusted to our care.

20God said, "Let the waters swarm with living things, and let birds fly above the earth up in the dome of the sky." 21God created the great sea animals and all the tiny living things that swarm in the waters, each according to its kind, and all the winged birds, each according to its kind. God saw how good it was. 22Then God blessed them: "Be fertile and multiply and fill the waters in the seas, and let the birds multiply on the earth."

23There was evening and there was morning: the fifth day.

24God said, "Let the earth produce every kind of living thing: livestock, crawling things, and wildlife." And that's what happened. 25God made every kind of wildlife, every kind of livestock, and every kind of creature that crawls on the ground. God saw how good it was. 26Then God said, "Let us make humanity in our image to resemble us so that they may take charge of the fish of the sea, the birds of the sky, the livestock, all the earth, and all the crawling things on earth."

[a]Or *In the beginning, God created*

105

If you looked up Luke 10:25-37, you found that the story of the Good Samaritan begins,
"A legal expert stood up. . . ."
This story ends,
"Jesus told him, 'Go and do likewise.' "
There are lots of good stories in the Bible.

In the Bible reference

LUKE 10:25-37,

you read from the beginning of verse ________ to the end of verse ________.

The hyphen (-) means that you read

_____ all of the verses between 25 and 37.

or

_____ none of the verses between 25 and 37.

(Check the right word.)

chapter

In the books of the Bible, the BIG numbers tell us where the

___ ___ ___ ___ ___ ___ ___ s

begin.

The LITTLE numbers tell us where the

___ ___ ___ ___ ___ s

begin.

World's creation in seven days

1 When God began to create[a] the heavens and
the earth— 2 the earth was without shape or
form, it was dark over the deep sea, and God's
wind swept over the waters— 3 God said, "Let
there be light." And so light appeared. 4 God
saw how good the light was. God separated
the light from the darkness. 5 God named the
light Day and the darkness Night.

There was evening and there was morning:
the first day.

LORD

LORD

If you would like, you can find a story that Jesus told. The story is called "The Good Samaritan."

The Bible reference is LUKE 10:25-37.

When you are finished reading this story (called a parable), turn to the next page.

68

chapters

verses

To make it easier to find a place in a book in the Bible,
most of the BOOKS of the Bible have been divided into large parts called

______________________.

Jesus studied the laws and rules of the Hebrew people in the Old Testament.

Find the most important rule of all:

DEUTERONOMY 6:4-5

Read the verses and write the missing words here:

"Israel, listen! Our God is the ______________! Only the ______________! Love the Lord your God with all your heart, all your being, and all your strength."

69

chapters

These chapters have been divided into smaller parts called

______________________.

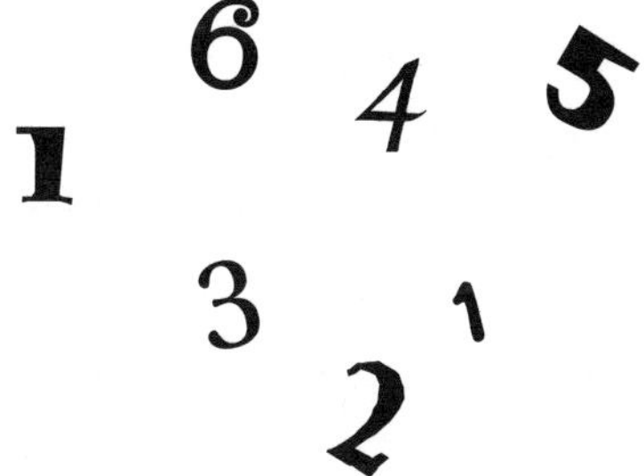

102

Luke 2

went

heart

Look in the Book of Matthew for some of Jesus' most famous teachings.

Find: MATTHEW 5:3-12

Look at these verses in your Bible.

Almost every verse begins with the same word. Write that word in this blank:

____

This list of teachings is called "The Beatitudes."

70

verses

We can find any CHAPTER we are looking for because each chapter has been given a:

_____ little number.

or a

_____ big number.

101

Story of the Word

1 In the beginning was the Word
and the Word was with God
and the Word was God.
2 The Word was with God
in the beginning.
3 Everything came into being
through the Word,
and without the Word
nothing came into being.
What came into being
4 through the Word was life,[a]
and the life was the light for all people.
5 The light shines in the darkness,
and the darkness doesn't
extinguish the light.
6 A man named John was sent from God.
7 He came as a witness to testify concerning
the light, so that through him everyone would
believe in the light. 8 He himself wasn't the
light, but his mission was to testify concerning the light.
9 The true light that shines on all people
was coming into the world.

Now see if you can find the story about Jesus going on a trip when he was twelve years old.

The Bible reference is LUKE 2:41-51.

First, find the Book of _______________, Chapter _________. After you find the big number 2, be sure you look DOWN the page and in the next column, or on the next page, until you find verse 41. (Some versions of the Bible make the verse easier to find than others do.)

Verse 41 begins, "Each year his parents __________ to Jerusalem. . . ."

Verse 51 ENDS with these words: "His mother cherished every word in her _______________."

71

big

We can find any Bible VERSE we are looking for because each verse has been given a:

_____ little number

or a

_____ big number.

100

Story of the Word

1 In the beginning was the Word
and the Word was with God
and the Word was God.
2 The Word was with God
in the beginning.
3 Everything came into being
through the Word,
and without the Word
nothing came into being.
What came into being
4 through the Word was life,[a]
and the life was the light for all people.
5 The light shines in the darkness,
and the darkness doesn't
extinguish the light.
6 A man named John was sent from God.
7 He came as a witness to testify concerning
the light, so that through him everyone would
believe in the light. 8 He himself wasn't the
light, but his mission was to testify concerning the light.
9 The true light that shines on all people
was coming into the world.

Suppose your teacher gives you the Bible reference

JOHN 1:6-8

(John one, six through eight).

On this picture, draw a line around verses 6 through 8.

Check again to see that you marked only three verses for reading!

Story of the Word

1 In the beginning was the Word
and the Word was with God
and the Word was God.
2 The Word was with God
in the beginning.
3 Everything came into being
through the Word,
and without the Word
nothing came into being.
What came into being
4 through the Word was life,[a]
and the life was the light for all people.
5 The light shines in the darkness,
and the darkness doesn't
extinguish the light.
6 A man named John was sent from God.
7 He came as a witness to testify concerning
the light, so that through him everyone would
believe in the light. 8 He himself wasn't the
light, but his mission was to testify concerning the light.
9 The true light that shines on all people
was coming into the world.

little

Check the right word.

The chapter numbers are:

_____ larger

or

_____ smaller

than the verse numbers.

In this picture of the first part of the Book of John, DRAW A CIRCLE around the CHAPTER number.

Story of the Word

1 In the beginning was the Word
and the Word was with God
and the Word was God.
2 The Word was with God
in the beginning.
3 Everything came into being
through the Word,
and without the Word
nothing came into being.
What came into being
4 through the Word was life,[a]
and the life was the light for all people.
5 The light shines in the darkness,
and the darkness doesn't
extinguish the light.
6 A man named John was sent from God.
7 He came as a witness to testify concerning
the light, so that through him everyone would
believe in the light. 8 He himself wasn't the
light, but his mission was to testify concerning the light.
9 The true light that shines on all people
was coming into the world.
10 The light was in the world,
and the world came into being
through the light,
but the world didn't recognize
the light.
11 The light came to his own people,
and his own people didn't welcome him.
12 But those who did welcome him,
those who believed in his name,
he authorized to become God's children,
13 born not from blood
nor from human desire or passion,
but born from God.
14 The Word became flesh
and made his home among us.
We have seen his glory,
glory like that of a father's only son,
full of grace and truth.
15 John testified about him, crying out,
"This is the one of whom I said, 'He who comes
after me is greater than me because he ex-
isted before me.'"
16 From his fullness we have all received
grace upon grace;
17 as the Law was given through Moses,

Bet you can read this in 30 seconds. Ready, set, go!

LIFE PRESERVER

What is "the Word"?

John 1:1-5

John is very different from Matthew, Mark, and Luke. John's Gospel was written later than the other three. John tells some different stories about Jesus and uses a lot of images like bread, water, light, and vines.

This book begins without a family tree (see Matthew), Jesus' baptism (see Mark), or a birth story (see Luke). Instead, it begins with the *Story of the Word*. John told his readers that Jesus is God's Word and work in the world. Jesus is God's presence in the world. God became human through the birth, life, death, and resurrection of Jesus. Then John shares stories that support his statement of who Jesus is.

so grace and truth came into being
through Jesus Christ.
18 No one has ever seen God.
God the only Son,
who is at the Father's side,
has made God known.

John's witness

19 This is John's testimony when the Jewish
leaders in Jerusalem sent priests and Levites
to ask him, "Who are you?"
20 John confessed (he didn't deny but confessed), "I'm not the Christ."
21 They asked him, "Then who are you? Are
you Elijah?"
John said, "I'm not."
"Are you the prophet?"
John answered, "No."
22 They asked, "Who are you? We need to
give an answer to those who sent us. What do
you say about yourself?"
23 John replied,
"I am a voice crying out in the wilderness.
Make the Lord's path straight,[b]
just as the prophet Isaiah said."
24 Those sent by the Pharisees 25 asked,
"Why do you baptize if you aren't the Christ,
nor Elijah, nor the prophet?"
26 John answered, "I baptize with water.

[a] Or *Everything came into being through the Word, / and without the Word / nothing came into being that came into being. In the Word was life* [b] Isa 40:3

end

Here is a picture of the beginning of Chapter 1 of the Book of John.

Suppose your teacher gives you the Bible reference

JOHN 1:1-5

(John one, one through five).

On this picture draw a line around verses 1 through 5.

Be careful!
Be sure you include
ALL of verses 1-5.

Story of the Word

1 In the beginning was the Word
and the Word was with God
and the Word was God.
2 The Word was with God
in the beginning.
3 Everything came into being
through the Word,
and without the Word
nothing came into being.
What came into being
4 through the Word was life,[a]
and the life was the light for all people.
5 The light shines in the darkness,
and the darkness doesn't
extinguish the light.
6 A man named John was sent from God.
7 He came as a witness to testify concerning
the light, so that through him everyone would
believe in the light. 8 He himself wasn't the
light, but his mission was to testify concerning the light.
9 The true light that shines on all people
was coming into the world.

larger

Story of the Word

1 In the beginning was the Word
and the Word was with God
and the Word was God.
2 The Word was with God
in the beginning.
3 Everything came into being
through the Word,
and without the Word
nothing came into being.
What came into being
4 through the Word was life,[a]
and the life was the light for all people.
5 The light shines in the darkness,
and the darkness doesn't
extinguish the light.
6 A man named John was sent from God.
7 He came as a witness to testify concerning
the light, so that through him everyone would
believe in the light. 8 He himself wasn't the
light, but his mission was to testify concerning the light.
9 The true light that shines on all people
was coming into the world.
10 The light was in the world,
and the world came into being
through the light,
but the world didn't recognize
the light.
11 The light came to his own people,
and his own people didn't welcome him.
12 But those who did welcome him,
those who believed in his name,
he authorized to become God's children,
13 born not from blood
nor from human desire or passion,
but born from God.
14 The Word became flesh
and made his home among us.
We have seen his glory,
glory like that of a father's only son,
full of grace and truth.
15 John testified about him, crying out,
"This is the one of whom I said, 'He who comes
after me is greater than me because he ex-
isted before me.'"
16 From his fullness we have all received
grace upon grace;
17 as the Law was given through Moses,

Bet you can read this in 30 seconds. Ready, set, go!

LIFE PRESERVER

What is "the Word"?

John is very different from Matthew, Mark, and Luke. John's Gospel was written later than the other three. John tells some different stories about Jesus and uses a lot of images like bread, water, light, and vines.

This book begins without a family tree (see Matthew), Jesus' baptism (see Mark), or a birth story (see Luke). Instead, it begins with the *Story of the Word*. John told his readers that Jesus is God's Word and work in the world. Jesus is God's presence in the world. God became human through the birth, life, death, and resurrection of Jesus. Then John shares stories that support his statement of who Jesus is.

so grace and truth came into being
through Jesus Christ.
18 No one has ever seen God.
God the only Son,
who is at the Father's side,
has made God known.

John's witness

19 This is John's testimony when the Jewish
leaders in Jerusalem sent priests and Levites
to ask him, "Who are you?"
20 John confessed (he didn't deny but confessed), "I'm not the Christ."
21 They asked him, "Then who are you? Are
you Elijah?"
John said, "I'm not."
"Are you the prophet?"
John answered, "No."
22 They asked, "Who are you? We need to
give an answer to those who sent us. What do
you say about yourself?"
23 John replied,
"*I am a voice crying out in the wilderness,*
Make the Lord's path straight,[b]
just as the prophet Isaiah said."
24 Those sent by the Pharisees 25 asked,
"Why do you baptize if you aren't the Christ,
nor Elijah, nor the prophet?"
26 John answered, "I baptize with water.

[a] Or *Everything came into being through the Word / and without the Word /* [illegible] *Word was life* [b] Isa 40:3

The verse numbers are:

_____ larger

or

_____ smaller

than the chapter numbers.

In this picture of the first part of the Book of John, draw a circle around EACH VERSE NUMBER. You should find EIGHT verse numbers in this picture.

Story of the Word

1 In the beginning was the Word
and the Word was with God
and the Word was God.
2 The Word was with God
in the beginning.
3 Everything came into being
through the Word,
and without the Word
nothing came into being.
What came into being
4 through the Word was life,[a]
and the life was the light for all people.
5 The light shines in the darkness,
and the darkness doesn't
extinguish the light.
6 A man named John was sent from God.
7 He came as a witness to testify concerning
the light, so that through him everyone would
believe in the light. 8 He himself wasn't the
light, but his mission was to testify concerning the light.
9 The true light that shines on all people
was coming into the world.

98

chapter

verse

verse

In the Bible reference

LUKE 2:1-20

you BEGIN reading at verse 1.

You STOP reading at the _____ beginning of verse 20.

or

the _____ end of verse 20.

(Check the right word.)

smaller

Story of the Word

1 In the beginning was the Word
and the Word was with God
and the Word was God.
2 The Word was with God
in the beginning.
3 Everything came into being
through the Word,
and without the Word
nothing came into being.
What came into being
4 through the Word was life,[a]
and the life was the light for all people.
5 The light shines in the darkness,
and the darkness doesn't
extinguish the light.
6 A man named John was sent from God.
7 He came as a witness to testify concerning
the light, so that through him everyone would
believe in the light. 8 He himself wasn't the
light, but his mission was to testify concerning the light.
9 The true light that shines on all people
was coming into the world.

A verse number tells where a verse begins.

A verse ends when you come to the next verse number or when you come to the end of a chapter.

In this picture, all the words of verse 7 are circled.

Now circle all the words of verse 4 in this picture.

Story of the Word

1 In the beginning was the Word
and the Word was with God
and the Word was God.
2 The Word was with God
in the beginning.
3 Everything came into being
through the Word,
and without the Word
nothing came into being.
What came into being
4 through the Word was life,[a]
and the life was the light for all people.
5 The light shines in the darkness,
and the darkness doesn't
extinguish the light.
6 A man named John was sent from God.
7 He came as a witness to testify concerning
the light, so that through him everyone would
believe in the light. 8 He himself wasn't the
light, but his mission was to testify concerning the light.
9 The true light that shines on all people
was coming into the world.

97

1 20

Check the right words.

In the Bible reference LUKE 2:1-20

the number 2 is a _____ chapter number

or

a _____ verse number

the number 1 is a _____ chapter number

or

a _____ verse number

the number 20 is a _____ chapter number

or

a _____ verse number

Story of the Word

1 In the beginning was the Word
and the Word was with God
and the Word was God.
2 The Word was with God
in the beginning.
3 Everything came into being
through the Word,
and without the Word
nothing came into being.
What came into being
4 through the Word was life,[a]
and the life was the light for all people.
5 The light shines in the darkness,
and the darkness doesn't
extinguish the light.
6 A man named John was sent from God.
7 He came as a witness to testify concerning
the light, so that through him everyone would
believe in the light. 8 He himself wasn't the
light, but his mission was to testify concerning the light.
9 The true light that shines on all people
was coming into the world.

Some Bibles include a timeline, often near the front of a Bible. A timeline can be a valuable resource because it tells you when certain events in the Bible happened.

If you can locate a timeline in your Bible, does it tell you the approximate year that Moses was born? ____________

Does your timeline tell you the approximate year the Israelites entered the Promised Land? ______________

Notice that the numbers are larger and then get smaller as they get closer to the birth of Jesus. After the birth of Jesus, the numbers go up again.

Does your timeline tell you when Pentecost was? __________

2 1

20

This little mark is called a hyphen (say, "HI fun").

In the Bible reference

LUKE 2:1-20

the hyphen (-) means that you READ ALL THE VERSES from verse __________ through verse __________.

About 1350 B.C.

About 1200 B.C.

After 30 A.D.

Turn in your Bible to the Book of Genesis and find Chapter 1.

You will find the BIG number 1 for Chapter 1, but you will not find the LITTLE number 1 for verse 1.

The number for VERSE 1 is not printed in most Bibles.

Do you think you can find the words of verse 1, even if the verse number is not printed there? _____ Yes _____ No

World's creation in seven days

1 When God began to create[a] the heavens and the earth— [2]the earth was without shape or form, it was dark over the deep sea, and God's wind swept over the waters— [3]God said, "Let there be light." And so light appeared. [4]God saw how good the light was. God separated the light from the darkness. [5]God named the light Day and the darkness Night.

There was evening and there was morning: the first day.

Matthew①: 18

But most of the time you will read more than one verse.

Suppose you see a reference like this:

LUKE 2:1-20

(SAY, "Luke two, one through twenty.")

This means that you are to find the Book of Luke, Chapter __________, and begin reading at verse __________. You keep on reading ALL the verses on through the END of verse __________.

Yes

Now turn in your Bible to the Book of John in the New Testament.

In the Bible, every chapter begins with verse 1, even if the number is not printed there.

Circle ALL the words of verse 1 in this picture.

Be careful! Circle only the words of VERSE 1.

Story of the Word

1 In the beginning was the Word
and the Word was with God
and the Word was God.
2 The Word was with God
in the beginning.
3 Everything came into being
through the Word,
and without the Word
nothing came into being.
What came into being
4 through the Word was life,[a]
and the life was the light for all people.
5 The light shines in the darkness,
and the darkness doesn't
extinguish the light.

1

18

In the Bible reference

MATTHEW 1:18

draw a square around the verse number.

Draw a circle around the chapter number.

This mark : is called a COLON.

Story of the Word

1 In the beginning was the Word
and the Word was with God
and the Word was God.
2 The Word was with God
in the beginning.
3 Everything came into being
through the Word,
and without the Word
nothing came into being.
What came into being
4 through the Word was life,[a]
and the life was the light for all people.
5 The light shines in the darkness,
and the darkness doesn't
extinguish the light.

In a Bible reference like John 3:16, the number after the name of the book is the CHAPTER number: John 3:16

The number after the (:) is the VERSE number.

In the reference

JOHN 3:16

the number 3 is the _____ verse number

or

the number 3 is the _____ chapter number.

Check the right word.

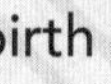

birth

In the Bible reference

MATTHEW 1:18

the chapter number is __________

the verse number is __________

If you found the verse in Matthew without any trouble, you are getting very good at looking up Bible references!

79

chapter

In the reference

JOHN 3:16

the number 16 is the _____ verse number

or

the number 16 is the _____ chapter number.

Let us look up another Bible reference.

Not all of the Christmas story is found in Luke. Another part of it begins with MATTHEW 1:18.

Find MATTHEW 1:18 in your Bible.

First, go to the Book of Matthew and find the BIG number 1. Then look DOWN the page until you find verse 18. You may have to look in the next column or even on the next page before you find the 18.

Matthew 1:18 begins: "This is how the ______________ of Jesus Christ took place. . . ."

80

verse

In the Bible reference
JOHN 3:16,
draw a circle around the CHAPTER number.

91

Luke

2 1

Look up the beginning of the Christmas story in your Bible.

The Bible reference is LUKE 2:1. Luke is in the New Testament.

After you find Luke, look for the big number 2. Verse 1 will not have a number, but you know it is at the beginning of Chapter 2.

The Christmas story in Luke begins:

"In those ______________ Caesar Augustus declared. . . ."

81

John③:16

In the Bible reference

JOHN 3:16,

draw a square around the VERSE number.

90

verses

The Christmas story begins with the FIRST VERSE of the SECOND CHAPTER of LUKE.

To make it shorter, you say that the Christmas story begins with LUKE 2:1.

(We SAY, "Luke two-one.")

If you want to read the Christmas story in the Bible, you will look for the book named _______________, then find chapter __________, and begin reading at verse __________.

82

John 3:16

References are written with a colon (:).

Some Bibles use periods with references (.)

Either way it means the same thing.

If you see a Bible reference like this:

John 1.4

what is another way of writing it? ________________

89

chapters

In the Bible, the CHAPTERS have been divided into small parts called ______________________________.

Here is a picture of Chapter 3 in the Book of John.

Find John 3:16 in your Bible.

Start with the big number 3 and look until you find the verse number 16. In some Bibles, you might find this verse in the next column.

Read ALL THE WORDS of John 3:16 in your Bible.

John 1:4

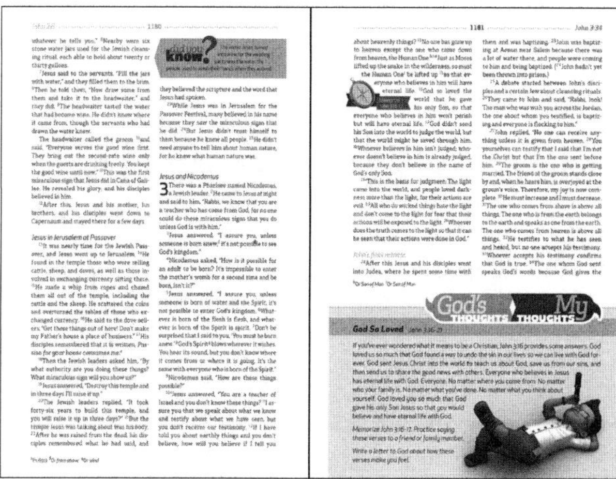

John 2:6 1180

whatever he tells you." [6]Nearby were six stone water jars used for the Jewish cleansing ritual, each able to hold about twenty or thirty gallons.

[7]Jesus said to the servants, "Fill the jars with water," and they filled them to the brim. [8]Then he told them, "Now draw some from them and take it to the headwaiter," and they did. [9]The headwaiter tasted the water that had become wine. He didn't know where it came from, though the servants who had drawn the water knew.

The headwaiter called the groom [10]and said, "Everyone serves the good wine first. They bring out the second-rate wine only when the guests are drinking freely. You kept the good wine until now." [11]This was the first miraculous sign that Jesus did in Cana of Galilee. He revealed his glory, and his disciples believed in him.

[12]After this, Jesus and his mother, his brothers, and his disciples went down to Capernaum and stayed there for a few days.

Jesus in Jerusalem at Passover

[13]It was nearly time for the Jewish Passover, and Jesus went up to Jerusalem. [14]He found in the temple those who were selling cattle, sheep, and doves, as well as those involved in exchanging currency sitting there. [15]He made a whip from ropes and chased them all out of the temple, including the cattle and the sheep. He scattered the coins and overturned the tables of those who exchanged currency. [16]He said to the dove sellers, "Get these things out of here! Don't make my Father's house a place of business." [17]His disciples remembered that it is written, *Passion for your house consumes me.*[a]

[18]Then the Jewish leaders asked him, "By what authority are you doing these things? What miraculous sign will you show us?"

[19]Jesus answered, "Destroy this temple and in three days I'll raise it up."

[20]The Jewish leaders replied, "It took forty-six years to build this temple, and you will raise it up in three days?" [21]But the temple Jesus was talking about was his body. [22]After he was raised from the dead, his disciples remembered what he had said, and

did you know?

they believed the scripture and the word that Jesus had spoken.

[23]While Jesus was in Jerusalem for the Passover Festival, many believed in his name because they saw the miraculous signs that he did. [24]But Jesus didn't trust himself to them because he knew all people. [25]He didn't need anyone to tell him about human nature, for he knew what human nature was.

Jesus and Nicodemus

3 There was a Pharisee named Nicodemus, a Jewish leader. [2]He came to Jesus at night and said to him, "Rabbi, we know that you are a teacher who has come from God, for no one could do these miraculous signs that you do unless God is with him."

[3]Jesus answered, "I assure you, unless someone is born anew,[b] it's not possible to see God's kingdom."

[4]Nicodemus asked, "How is it possible for an adult to be born? It's impossible to enter the mother's womb for a second time and be born, isn't it?"

[5]Jesus answered, "I assure you, unless someone is born of water and the Spirit, it's not possible to enter God's kingdom. [6]Whatever is born of the flesh is flesh, and whatever is born of the Spirit is spirit. [7]Don't be surprised that I said to you, 'You must be born anew.' [8]God's Spirit[c] blows wherever it wishes. You hear its sound, but you don't know where it comes from or where it is going. It's the same with everyone who is born of the Spirit."

[9]Nicodemus said, "How are these things possible?"

[10]Jesus answered, "You are a teacher of Israel and you don't know these things? [11]I assure you that we speak about what we know and testify about what we have seen, but you don't receive our testimony. [12]If I have told you about earthly things and you don't believe, how will you believe if I tell you

[a]Ps 69:9 [b]Or *from above* [c]Or *wind*

1181 John 3:34

about heavenly things? [13]No one has gone up to heaven except the one who came down from heaven, the Human One.[d] [14]Just as Moses lifted up the snake in the wilderness, so must the Human One[e] be lifted up [15]so that everyone who believes in him will have eternal life. [16]God so loved the world that he gave his only Son, so that everyone who believes in him won't perish but will have eternal life. [17]God didn't send his Son into the world to judge the world, but that the world might be saved through him. [18]Whoever believes in him isn't judged; whoever doesn't believe in him is already judged, because they don't believe in the name of God's only Son.

[19]"This is the basis for judgment: The light came into the world, and people loved darkness more than the light, for their actions are evil. [20]All who do wicked things hate the light and don't come to the light for fear that their actions will be exposed to the light. [21]Whoever does the truth comes to the light so that it can be seen that their actions were done in God."

John's final witness

[22]After this Jesus and his disciples went into Judea, where he spent some time with them and was baptizing. [23]John was baptizing at Aenon near Salem because there was a lot of water there, and people were coming to him and being baptized. ([24]John hadn't yet been thrown into prison.)

[25]A debate started between John's disciples and a certain Jew about cleansing rituals. [26]They came to John and said, "Rabbi, look! The man who was with you across the Jordan, the one about whom you testified, is baptizing and everyone is flocking to him."

[27]John replied, "No one can receive anything unless it is given from heaven. [28]You yourselves can testify that I said that I'm not the Christ but that I'm the one sent before him. [29]The groom is the one who is getting married. The friend of the groom stands close by and, when he hears him, is overjoyed at the groom's voice. Therefore, my joy is now complete. [30]He must increase and I must decrease. [31]The one who comes from above is above all things. The one who is from the earth belongs to the earth and speaks as one from the earth. The one who comes from heaven is above all things. [32]He testifies to what he has seen and heard, but no one accepts his testimony. [33]Whoever accepts his testimony confirms that God is true. [34]The one whom God sent speaks God's words because God gives the

[d]Or *Son of Man* [e]Or *Son of Man*

God's THOUGHTS / My THOUGHTS

God So Loved John 3:16-21

If you've ever wondered what it means to be a Christian, John 3:16 provides some answers. God loved us so much that God found a way to undo the sin in our lives so we can live with God forever. God sent Jesus Christ into the world to teach us about God, save us from our sins, and then send us to share the good news with others. Everyone who believes in Jesus has eternal life with God. Everyone. No matter where you come from. No matter who your family is. No matter what you've done. No matter what you think about yourself. God loved you so much that God gave his only Son Jesus so that you would believe and have eternal life with God.

Memorize John 3:16-17. Practice saying these verses to a friend or family member.

Write a letter to God about how these verses make you feel.

88

Many words can go in the blank—whatever makes sense.

find things
look up things
find verses
look up references

(Or something that means the same thing.)

In the Bible, most of the BOOKS have been divided into large parts called ______________________.

about heavenly things? 13No one has gone up
to heaven except the one who came down
from heaven, the Human One.[h] 14Just as Moses
lifted up the snake in the wilderness, so must
the Human One[i] be lifted up 15so that everyone who believes in him will have
eternal life. 16God so loved the
world that he gave
his only Son, so that
everyone who believes in him won't perish
but will have eternal life. 17God didn't send
his Son into the world to judge the world, but
that the world might be saved through him.
18Whoever believes in him isn't judged; whoever doesn't believe in him is already judged,
because they don't believe in the name of
God's only Son.
19"This is the basis for judgment: The light
came into the world, and people loved darkness more than the light, for their actions are
evil. 20All who do wicked things hate the light
and don't come to the light for fear that their
actions will be exposed to the light. 21Whoever
does the truth comes to the light so that it can
be seen that their actions were done in God."

John's final witness

22After this Jesus and his disciples went
into Judea, where he spent some time with
them and was baptizing. 23John was baptizing at Aenon near Salem because there was
a lot of water there, and people were coming
to him and being baptized. (24John hadn't yet
been thrown into prison.)
25A debate started between John's disciples and a certain Jew about cleansing rituals.
26They came to John and said, "Rabbi, look!
The man who was with you across the Jordan,
the one about whom you testified, is baptizing and everyone is flocking to him."
27John replied, "No one can receive anything unless it is given from heaven. 28You
yourselves can testify that I said that I'm not
the Christ but that I'm the one sent before
him. 29The groom is the one who is getting
married. The friend of the groom stands close
by and, when he hears him, is overjoyed at the
groom's voice. Therefore, my joy is now complete. 30He must increase and I must decrease.
31The one who comes from above is above all
things. The one who is from the earth belongs
to the earth and speaks as one from the earth.
The one who comes from heaven is above all
things. 32He testifies to what he has seen
and heard, but no one accepts his testimony.
33Whoever accepts his testimony confirms
that God is true. 34The one whom God sent
speaks God's words because God gives the

[h] Or *Son of Man* [i] Or *Son of Man*

God So Loved *John 3:16-21*

If you've ever wondered what it means to be a Christian, John 3:16 provides some answers. God loved us so much that God found a way to undo the sin in our lives so we can live with God forever. God sent Jesus Christ into the world to teach us about God, save us from our sins, and then send us to share the good news with others. Everyone who believes in Jesus has eternal life with God. Everyone. No matter where you come from. No matter who your family is. No matter what you've done. No matter what you think about yourself. God loved *you* so much that God gave his only Son Jesus so that *you* would believe and have eternal life with God.

Memorize John 3:16-17. Practice saying these verses to a friend or family member.

Write a letter to God about how these verses make you feel.

If your teacher says, "Matthew two-one," or writes Matthew 2:1, he or she means:

the Book of ____________________

chapter ____________________

verse ____________________

Put a word or a number in each blank.

Remember, now you read only the pages numbered after page 88.

Most of the books of the Bible have been divided into chapters, and the chapters have been divided into verses to make it easier to ______________________________ in the Bible.

Matthew

2

1

Time to rest!

When you are ready to go again, turn the page.

Then turn the book upside down and read those pages.
(Begin with page 87.)

God is with us and always hears our prayers. Sometimes when we pray, we use our bodies to express the feelings behind our words. Here are some different positions, or postures, that you can use when you pray!